Self (Ceremony)

poems by

Robert Balun

Finishing Line Press
Georgetown, Kentucky

Self (Ceremony)

Copyright © 2016 by Robert Balun
ISBN 978-1-944251-49-9 First Edition
All rights reserved under International and Pan-American Copyright Conventions.
No part of this book may be reproduced in any manner whatsoever without written
permission from the publisher, except in the case of brief quotations embodied in critical
articles and reviews.

ACKNOWLEDGMENTS

Thank you to the editors of *Bodega* and *Almost Five Quarterly*, who first published versions of these poems.

Thank you.

Editor: Christen Kincaid

Cover Art: Bianca Boragi

Author Photo: Bianca Boragi

Cover Design: Elizabeth Maines

Printed in the USA on acid-free paper.
Order online: www.finishinglinepress.com
          also available on amazon.com

                    Author inquiries and mail orders:
                          Finishing Line Press
                             P. O. Box 1626
                        Georgetown, Kentucky 40324
                                U. S. A.

Table of Contents

it's easy to disappear	pg. 1
remember to	pg. 2
I keep me in keepsakes	pg. 3
I have to remember my keys	pg. 4
remember to project this life	pg. 5
you said you	pg. 6
bloom and bring me	pg. 7
we can't see the neighbors	pg. 8
in the backyard shadow	pg. 9
you cover your mouth and I	pg. 10
days waver in	pg. 11
I let color	pg. 12
the body resolves	pg. 13
unmoored/post-hope	pg. 14

> *"I am losing my because.*
> *I said I was*
> *the new species: no one."*
>
> —*Alice Notley*

Self (Ceremony)

it's easy to disappear
here or there

I don't remember
            exactly I
look for the luster of best years—

      did I finish telling you what I was singing before—

remember to

        cover up what needs to be covered
construct sacred objects
            essential motion
resonance and recurrence—

        wrapped / in a code
        a pattern to keep

            hidden all day

I paste peals of remember

I keep me in keepsakes

        icon totems of
        mirrored gaze

inside the skull
analogy

        ruined spacial
        echo chamber

you smell like the sunset

        you smell like the dusk

and I always forget
how you fit in my hands—

        before this name erases the other
put it in your pocket

I have to remember my keys
who I am in each lock

      my mirror symmetry

      absorb today
      and pray into a cup for rain

put on some noise
put some asleep inside me—

remember to project this life
each repetition of the same
           same hungry eyed
     happy exercise
           the myths you make to fill each day—

           and maybe soon we'll reach the other
           this prayer we've been digging up
that sunlight totem we left inside—

     a story that goes

           exactly how it is supposed to
into and then out of render—

     smoke or song
     hanging like rain—

     the shape of uncertainty

you said you

had seven
bottles of time

    a cigarette
    and a dead ship
    sailing your fey mouth—

    we look to the door for recognition

my cup dissolves into a bubble of spectrum
please bring me back some rain

bloom and bring me

ritual newness

    spirit deal

I want

    something to carry—

    inside the collapsing weather / rushing through the window
and everything's been all wavy since—

we can't see the neighbors
but we can hear their guns

I do a version of this noise

        I call it the branch of science that studies a perfect movie

            the hero is a hero / the flag is a memorial

        let's go get stung by bees after this
        let's sew ourselves into the memory / a song

            you write / the equation of never sleeping

        a mouth blooming
        feathers plume
        tongued practice

I get like this

        because sentiments are dangerous
because I don't want you to feel ancient
        because we met in a dream bought with borrow

in the backyard shadow

I sit and listen to

        the neighborhood flung against the looping night

there is an emergency outside

a droning song
we spill our secrets to

        your story
        wrapped up
        in mine

        you cover your mouth and I
        want to cover mine

because I need the echo

           line and shadow
           cast through the window

days waver in

    static and sometimes

    there is
    the noise of
    a soft dancing in the other room

    a twostep
    you fill—

I let color

    leak out

through the weak parts of skin

    a kaleidoscopic hole in my hand

the body resolves
for a time
as wavelength

an identity of light

and when these days are gone
you will not remember
the feeling of never
knowing they would ever go—

　　　　　unmoored / post-hope
　　you reach up and pluck
　　　　　the sky resonates
　　　　　　　　I look for time

I defined as imaginary unit
　　　　　　as matter
　　　　drifts into
ribbons of light—

Robert Balun received his MFA from The City College of New York, where he was a recipient of the Jerome Lowell DeJur Prize for Poetry and the Teacher-Writer Award. His poems have appeared in *Cosmonauts Avenue, Bodega, Smoking Glue Gun, Heavy Feather Review, Word Riot, Verdad Magazine,* and others. He teaches creative writing and composition at The City College of New York. Find him online at www.robertbalun.com

www.ingramcontent.com/pod-product-compliance
Lightning Source LLC
Chambersburg PA
CBHW060228050426
42446CB00013B/3219